MINI PASSWORD NOTEBOOK

"Password Log Book And Internet Password Organizer"

THIS BOOK BELONGS TO

SOFTWARE INFORMATION

Software: _______________________
Purchase Date: _______________________
License Key: _______________________
____

Software: _______________________
Purchase Date: _______________________
License Key: _______________________
____

Software: _______________________
Purchase Date: _______________________
License Key: _______________________
____

Software: _______________________
Purchase Date: _______________________
License Key: _______________________
____

Software: _______________________
Purchase Date: _______________________
License Key: _______________________
____

COMPUTER INFORMATION

Computer #1: _______________

Model: _______________

Serial Number: _______________

Purchase Date: _______________

Warranty: _______________

Support: _______________

Notes: _______________

Computer #2: _______________

Model: _______________

Serial Number: _______________

Purchase Date: _______________

Warranty: _______________

Support: _______________

Notes: _______________

Computer #3: _______________

Model: _______________

Serial Number: _______________

Purchase Date: _______________

Warranty: _______________

Support: _______________

Notes: _______________

NETWORK INFORMATION #1

ISP Name: _______________________

Website: _______________________

Account Number: _______________________

Email: _______________________

Password: _______________________

Support: _______________________

Notes: _______________________

____

Modem/Router: _______________________

Model: _______________________

Serial Number: _______________________

Admin URL: _______________________

Username: _______________________

Password: _______________________

Notes: _______________________

____

SSID (WiFi Network Name): _______________________

Password: _______________________

Security Mode: _______________________

Notes: _______________________

____

NETWORK INFORMATION #2

ISP Name:

Website:

Account Number:

Email:

Password:

Support:

Notes:

Modem/Router:

Model:

Serial Number:

Admin URL:

Username:

Password:

Notes:

SSID (WiFi Network Name):

Password:

Security Mode:

Notes:

Website:

Email:

Username:

Date/Password:

Date/Password:

Date/Password:

Notes:

Website:

Email:

Username:

Date/Password:

Date/Password:

Date/Password:

Notes:

Website:

Email:

Username:

Date/Password:

Date/Password:

Date/Password:

Notes:

Website:

Email:

Username:

Date/Password:

Date/Password:

Date/Password:

Notes:

Website:

Email:

Username:

Date/Password:

Date/Password:

Date/Password:

Notes:

Website:

Email:

Username:

Date/Password:

Date/Password:

Date/Password:

Notes:

A

Website: _______________________________________
Email: _______________________________________
Username: _______________________________________
Date/Password: _______________________________________
Date/Password: _______________________________________
Date/Password: _______________________________________
Notes: _______________________________________
____

Website: _______________________________________
Email: _______________________________________
Username: _______________________________________
Date/Password: _______________________________________
Date/Password: _______________________________________
Date/Password: _______________________________________
Notes: _______________________________________
____

Website: _______________________________________
Email: _______________________________________
Username: _______________________________________
Date/Password: _______________________________________
Date/Password: _______________________________________
Date/Password: _______________________________________
Notes: _______________________________________
____

Website:

Email:

Username:

Date/Password:

Date/Password:

Date/Password:

Notes:

Website:

Email:

Username:

Date/Password:

Date/Password:

Date/Password:

Notes:

Website:

Email:

Username:

Date/Password:

Date/Password:

Date/Password:

Notes:

Website:

Email:

Username:

Date/Password:

Date/Password:

Date/Password:

Notes:

Website:

Email:

Username:

Date/Password:

Date/Password:

Date/Password:

Notes:

Website:

Email:

Username:

Date/Password:

Date/Password:

Date/Password:

Notes:

Website:

Email:

Username:

Date/Password:

Date/Password:

Date/Password:

Notes:

B

Website:

Email:

Username:

Date/Password:

Date/Password:

Date/Password:

Notes:

Website:

Email:

Username:

Date/Password:

Date/Password:

Date/Password:

Notes:

Website: _______________________________
Email: _______________________________
Username: _______________________________
Date/Password: _______________________________
Date/Password: _______________________________
Date/Password: _______________________________
Notes: _______________________________
____

Website: _______________________________
Email: _______________________________
Username: _______________________________
Date/Password: _______________________________
Date/Password: _______________________________
Date/Password: _______________________________
Notes: _______________________________
____

Website: _______________________________
Email: _______________________________
Username: _______________________________
Date/Password: _______________________________
Date/Password: _______________________________
Date/Password: _______________________________
Notes: _______________________________
____

Website:

Email:

Username:

Date/Password:

Date/Password:

Date/Password:

Notes:

Website:

Email:

Username:

Date/Password:

Date/Password:

Date/Password:

Notes:

Website:

Email:

Username:

Date/Password:

Date/Password:

Date/Password:

Notes:

C

Website:

Email:

Username:

Date/Password:

Date/Password:

Date/Password:

Notes:

Website:

Email:

Username:

Date/Password:

Date/Password:

Date/Password:

Notes:

Website:

Email:

Username:

Date/Password:

Date/Password:

Date/Password:

Notes:

Website:

Email:

Username:

Date/Password:

Date/Password:

Date/Password:

Notes:

Website:

Email:

Username:

Date/Password:

Date/Password:

Date/Password:

Notes:

Website:

Email:

Username:

Date/Password:

Date/Password:

Date/Password:

Notes:

Website:

Email:

Username:

Date/Password:

Date/Password:

Date/Password:

Notes:

Website:

Email:

Username:

Date/Password:

Date/Password:

Date/Password:

Notes:

Website:

Email:

Username:

Date/Password:

Date/Password:

Date/Password:

Notes:

Website:

Email:

Username:

Date/Password:

Date/Password:

Date/Password:

Notes:

Website:

Email:

Username:

Date/Password:

Date/Password:

Date/Password:

Notes:

Website:

Email:

Username:

Date/Password:

Date/Password:

Date/Password:

Notes:

D

Website: _______________________

Email: _______________________

Username: _______________________

Date/Password: _______________________

Date/Password: _______________________

Date/Password: _______________________

Notes: _______________________

____

Website: _______________________

Email: _______________________

Username: _______________________

Date/Password: _______________________

Date/Password: _______________________

Date/Password: _______________________

Notes: _______________________

____

Website: _______________________

Email: _______________________

Username: _______________________

Date/Password: _______________________

Date/Password: _______________________

Date/Password: _______________________

Notes: _______________________

____

Website:

Email:

Username:

Date/Password:

Date/Password:

Date/Password:

Notes:

Website:

Email:

Username:

Date/Password:

Date/Password:

Date/Password:

Notes:

Website:

Email:

Username:

Date/Password:

Date/Password:

Date/Password:

Notes:

D

Website:

Email:

Username:

Date/Password:

Date/Password:

Date/Password:

Notes:

Website:

Email:

Username:

Date/Password:

Date/Password:

Date/Password:

Notes:

Website:

Email:

Username:

Date/Password:

Date/Password:

Date/Password:

Notes:

Website:

Email:

Username:

Date/Password:

Date/Password:

Date/Password:

Notes:

Website:

Email:

Username:

Date/Password:

Date/Password:

Date/Password:

Notes:

Website:

Email:

Username:

Date/Password:

Date/Password:

Date/Password:

Notes:

Website:

Email:

Username:

Date/Password:

Date/Password:

Date/Password:

Notes:

Website:

Email:

Username:

Date/Password:

Date/Password:

Date/Password:

Notes:

Website:

Email:

Username:

Date/Password:

Date/Password:

Date/Password:

Notes:

Website:

Email:

Username:

Date/Password:

Date/Password:

Date/Password:

Notes:

Website:

Email:

Username:

Date/Password:

Date/Password:

Date/Password:

Notes:

Website:

Email:

Username:

Date/Password:

Date/Password:

Date/Password:

Notes:

Website: _______________________
Email: _______________________
Username: _______________________
Date/Password: _______________________
Date/Password: _______________________
Date/Password: _______________________
Notes: _______________________
____

Website: _______________________
Email: _______________________
Username: _______________________
Date/Password: _______________________
Date/Password: _______________________
Date/Password: _______________________
Notes: _______________________
____

Website: _______________________
Email: _______________________
Username: _______________________
Date/Password: _______________________
Date/Password: _______________________
Date/Password: _______________________
Notes: _______________________
____

Website:____

Email:____

Username:____

Date/Password:____

Date/Password:____

Date/Password:____

Notes:____

____

Website:____

Email:____

Username:____

Date/Password:____

Date/Password:____

Date/Password:____

Notes:____

____

Website:____

Email:____

Username:____

Date/Password:____

Date/Password:____

Date/Password:____

Notes:____

____

Website:

Email:

Username:

Date/Password:

Date/Password:

Date/Password:

Notes:

Website:

Email:

Username:

Date/Password:

Date/Password:

Date/Password:

Notes:

Website:

Email:

Username:

Date/Password:

Date/Password:

Date/Password:

Notes:

Website:

Email:

Username:

Date/Password:

Date/Password:

Date/Password:

Notes:

Website:

Email:

Username:

Date/Password:

Date/Password:

Date/Password:

Notes:

Website:

Email:

Username:

Date/Password:

Date/Password:

Date/Password:

Notes:

F

Website:

Email:

Username:

Date/Password:

Date/Password:

Date/Password:

Notes:

Website:

Email:

Username:

Date/Password:

Date/Password:

Date/Password:

Notes:

Website:

Email:

Username:

Date/Password:

Date/Password:

Date/Password:

Notes:

Website:

Email:

Username:

Date/Password:

Date/Password:

Date/Password:

Notes:

F

Website:

Email:

Username:

Date/Password:

Date/Password:

Date/Password:

Notes:

Website:

Email:

Username:

Date/Password:

Date/Password:

Date/Password:

Notes:

Website:

Email:

Username:

Date/Password:

Date/Password:

Date/Password:

Notes:

Website:

Email:

Username:

Date/Password:

Date/Password:

Date/Password:

Notes:

Website:

Email:

Username:

Date/Password:

Date/Password:

Date/Password:

Notes:

Website:

Email:

Username:

Date/Password:

Date/Password:

Date/Password:

Notes:

G

Website:

Email:

Username:

Date/Password:

Date/Password:

Date/Password:

Notes:

Website:

Email:

Username:

Date/Password:

Date/Password:

Date/Password:

Notes:

Website: _______________
Email: _______________
Username: _______________
Date/Password: _______________
Date/Password: _______________
Date/Password: _______________
Notes: _______________
____

Website: _______________
Email: _______________
Username: _______________
Date/Password: _______________
Date/Password: _______________
Date/Password: _______________
Notes: _______________
____

Website: _______________
Email: _______________
Username: _______________
Date/Password: _______________
Date/Password: _______________
Date/Password: _______________
Notes: _______________
____

Website:

Email:

Username:

Date/Password:

Date/Password:

Date/Password:

Notes:

G

Website:

Email:

Username:

Date/Password:

Date/Password:

Date/Password:

Notes:

Website:

Email:

Username:

Date/Password:

Date/Password:

Date/Password:

Notes:

H

Website: ___________________________________

Email: ___________________________________

Username: ___________________________________

Date/Password: ___________________________________

Date/Password: ___________________________________

Date/Password: ___________________________________

Notes: ___________________________________

____

Website: ___________________________________

Email: ___________________________________

Username: ___________________________________

Date/Password: ___________________________________

Date/Password: ___________________________________

Date/Password: ___________________________________

Notes: ___________________________________

____

Website: ___________________________________

Email: ___________________________________

Username: ___________________________________

Date/Password: ___________________________________

Date/Password: ___________________________________

Date/Password: ___________________________________

Notes: ___________________________________

____

Website:

Email:

Username:

Date/Password:

Date/Password:

Date/Password:

Notes:

Website:

Email:

Username:

Date/Password:

Date/Password:

Date/Password:

Notes:

Website:

Email:

Username:

Date/Password:

Date/Password:

Date/Password:

Notes:

Website: ____

Email: ____

Username: ____

Date/Password: ____

Date/Password: ____

Date/Password: ____

Notes: ____

____

Website: ____

Email: ____

Username: ____

Date/Password: ____

Date/Password: ____

Date/Password: ____

Notes: ____

____

Website: ____

Email: ____

Username: ____

Date/Password: ____

Date/Password: ____

Date/Password: ____

Notes: ____

____

Website: _______________________

Email: _______________________

Username: _______________________

Date/Password: _______________________

Date/Password: _______________________

Date/Password: _______________________

Notes: _______________________

____

Website: _______________________

Email: _______________________

Username: _______________________

Date/Password: _______________________

Date/Password: _______________________

Date/Password: _______________________

Notes: _______________________

____

Website: _______________________

Email: _______________________

Username: _______________________

Date/Password: _______________________

Date/Password: _______________________

Date/Password: _______________________

Notes: _______________________

____

Website:

Email:

Username:

Date/Password:

Date/Password:

Date/Password:

Notes:

Website:

Email:

Username:

Date/Password:

Date/Password:

Date/Password:

Notes:

Website:

Email:

Username:

Date/Password:

Date/Password:

Date/Password:

Notes:

Website:

Email:

Username:

Date/Password:

Date/Password:

Date/Password:

Notes:

Website:

Email:

Username:

Date/Password:

Date/Password:

Date/Password:

Notes:

Website:

Email:

Username:

Date/Password:

Date/Password:

Date/Password:

Notes:

Website:

Email:

Username:

Date/Password:

Date/Password:

Date/Password:

Notes:

Website:

Email:

Username:

Date/Password:

Date/Password:

Date/Password:

Notes:

Website:

Email:

Username:

Date/Password:

Date/Password:

Date/Password:

Notes:

Website:

Email:

Username:

Date/Password:

Date/Password:

Date/Password:

Notes:

Website:

Email:

Username:

Date/Password:

Date/Password:

Date/Password:

Notes:

Website:

Email:

Username:

Date/Password:

Date/Password:

Date/Password:

Notes:

Website:

Email:

Username:

Date/Password:

Date/Password:

Date/Password:

Notes:

J

Website:

Email:

Username:

Date/Password:

Date/Password:

Date/Password:

Notes:

Website:

Email:

Username:

Date/Password:

Date/Password:

Date/Password:

Notes:

Website:

Email:

Username:

Date/Password:

Date/Password:

Date/Password:

Notes:

Website:

Email:

Username:

Date/Password:

Date/Password:

Date/Password:

Notes:

Website:

Email:

Username:

Date/Password:

Date/Password:

Date/Password:

Notes:

J

Website: ___________________________________
Email: _____________________________________
Username: __________________________________
Date/Password: _____________________________
Date/Password: _____________________________
Date/Password: _____________________________
Notes: _____________________________________
____

Website: ___________________________________
Email: _____________________________________
Username: __________________________________
Date/Password: _____________________________
Date/Password: _____________________________
Date/Password: _____________________________
Notes: _____________________________________
____

Website: ___________________________________
Email: _____________________________________
Username: __________________________________
Date/Password: _____________________________
Date/Password: _____________________________
Date/Password: _____________________________
Notes: _____________________________________
____

Website:

Email:

Username:

Date/Password:

Date/Password:

Date/Password:

Notes:

Website:

Email:

Username:

Date/Password:

Date/Password:

Date/Password:

Notes:

Website:

Email:

Username:

Date/Password:

Date/Password:

Date/Password:

Notes:

Website:

Email:

Username:

Date/Password:

Date/Password:

Date/Password:

Notes:

Website:

Email:

Username:

Date/Password:

Date/Password:

Date/Password:

Notes:

Website:

Email:

Username:

Date/Password:

Date/Password:

Date/Password:

Notes:

Website: _______________________________

Email: _______________________________

Username: _______________________________

Date/Password: _______________________________

Date/Password: _______________________________

Date/Password: _______________________________

Notes: _______________________________

____

Website: _______________________________

Email: _______________________________

Username: _______________________________

Date/Password: _______________________________

Date/Password: _______________________________

Date/Password: _______________________________

Notes: _______________________________

____

K

Website: _______________________________

Email: _______________________________

Username: _______________________________

Date/Password: _______________________________

Date/Password: _______________________________

Date/Password: _______________________________

Notes: _______________________________

____

Website:

Email:

Username:

Date/Password:

Date/Password:

Date/Password:

Notes:

Website:

Email:

Username:

Date/Password:

Date/Password:

Date/Password:

Notes:

Website:

Email:

Username:

Date/Password:

Date/Password:

Date/Password:

Notes:

Website:

Email:

Username:

Date/Password:

Date/Password:

Date/Password:

Notes:

Website:

Email:

Username:

Date/Password:

Date/Password:

Date/Password:

Notes:

Website:

Email:

Username:

Date/Password:

Date/Password:

Date/Password:

Notes:

L

Website:
Email:
Username:
Date/Password:
Date/Password:
Date/Password:
Notes:

Website:
Email:
Username:
Date/Password:
Date/Password:
Date/Password:
Notes:

Website:
Email:
Username:
Date/Password:
Date/Password:
Date/Password:
Notes:

Website:

Email:

Username:

Date/Password:

Date/Password:

Date/Password:

Notes:

Website:

Email:

Username:

Date/Password:

Date/Password:

Date/Password:

Notes:

Website:

Email:

Username:

Date/Password:

Date/Password:

Date/Password:

Notes:

Website:

Email:

Username:

Date/Password:

Date/Password:

Date/Password:

Notes:

Website:

Email:

Username:

Date/Password:

Date/Password:

Date/Password:

Notes:

Website:

Email:

Username:

Date/Password:

Date/Password:

Date/Password:

Notes:

Website: ____

Email: ____

Username: ____

Date/Password: ____

Date/Password: ____

Date/Password: ____

Notes: ____

____

Website: ____

Email: ____

Username: ____

Date/Password: ____

Date/Password: ____

Date/Password: ____

Notes: ____

____

Website: ____

Email: ____

Username: ____

Date/Password: ____

Date/Password: ____

Date/Password: ____

Notes: ____

____

Website:

Email:

Username:

Date/Password:

Date/Password:

Date/Password:

Notes:

Website:

Email:

Username:

M

Date/Password:

Date/Password:

Date/Password:

Notes:

Website:

Email:

Username:

Date/Password:

Date/Password:

Date/Password:

Notes:

Website:

Email:

Username:

Date/Password:

Date/Password:

Date/Password:

Notes:

Website:

Email:

Username:

Date/Password:

Date/Password:

Date/Password:

Notes:

Website:

Email:

Username:

Date/Password:

Date/Password:

Date/Password:

Notes:

M

Website:

Email:

Username:

Date/Password:

Date/Password:

Date/Password:

Notes:

Website:

Email:

Username:

Date/Password:

Date/Password:

Date/Password:

Notes:

Website:

Email:

Username:

Date/Password:

Date/Password:

Date/Password:

Notes:

Website: _______________________

Email: _______________________

Username: _______________________

Date/Password: _______________________

Date/Password: _______________________

Date/Password: _______________________

Notes: _______________________

____

Website: _______________________

Email: _______________________

Username: _______________________

Date/Password: _______________________

Date/Password: _______________________

Date/Password: _______________________

Notes: _______________________

____

Website: _______________________

Email: _______________________

Username: _______________________

Date/Password: _______________________

Date/Password: _______________________

Date/Password: _______________________

Notes: _______________________

____

Website:

Email:

Username:

Date/Password:

Date/Password:

Date/Password:

Notes:

Website:

Email:

Username:

Date/Password:

Date/Password:

Date/Password:

Notes:

Website:

Email:

Username:

Date/Password:

Date/Password:

Date/Password:

Notes:

Website:

Email:

Username:

Date/Password:

Date/Password:

Date/Password:

Notes:

Website:

Email:

Username:

Date/Password:

Date/Password:

Date/Password:

Notes:

Website:

Email:

Username:

Date/Password:

Date/Password:

Date/Password:

Notes:

Website:

Email:

Username:

Date/Password:

Date/Password:

Date/Password:

Notes:

Website:

Email:

Username:

Date/Password:

Date/Password:

Date/Password:

Notes:

Website:

Email:

Username:

Date/Password:

Date/Password:

Date/Password:

Notes:

Website:

Email:

Username:

Date/Password:

Date/Password:

Date/Password:

Notes:

Website:

Email:

Username:

Date/Password:

Date/Password:

Date/Password:

Notes:

Website:

Email:

Username:

Date/Password:

Date/Password:

Date/Password:

Notes:

Website:

Email:

Username:

Date/Password:

Date/Password:

Date/Password:

Notes:

Website:

Email:

Username:

Date/Password:

Date/Password:

Date/Password:

Notes:

Website:

Email:

Username:

Date/Password:

Date/Password:

Date/Password:

Notes:

Website: _______________________________

Email: _______________________________

Username: _______________________________

Date/Password: _______________________________

Date/Password: _______________________________

Date/Password: _______________________________

Notes: _______________________________

____

Website: _______________________________

Email: _______________________________

Username: _______________________________

Date/Password: _______________________________

Date/Password: _______________________________

Date/Password: _______________________________

Notes: _______________________________

____

Website: _______________________________

Email: _______________________________

Username: _______________________________

Date/Password: _______________________________

Date/Password: _______________________________

Date/Password: _______________________________

Notes: _______________________________

____

Website:_______________________________

Email:_______________________________

Username:_______________________________

Date/Password:_______________________________

Date/Password:_______________________________

Date/Password:_______________________________

Notes:_______________________________

____

Website:_______________________________

Email:_______________________________

Username:_______________________________

Date/Password:_______________________________

Date/Password:_______________________________

Date/Password:_______________________________

Notes:_______________________________

____

Website:_______________________________

Email:_______________________________

Username:_______________________________

Date/Password:_______________________________

Date/Password:_______________________________

Date/Password:_______________________________

Notes:_______________________________

____

Website:

Email:

Username:

Date/Password:

Date/Password:

Date/Password:

Notes:

Website:

Email:

Username:

Date/Password:

Date/Password:

Date/Password:

Notes:

Website:

Email:

Username:

Date/Password:

Date/Password:

Date/Password:

Notes:

Website:

Email:

Username:

Date/Password:

Date/Password:

Date/Password:

Notes:

Website:

Email:

Username:

Date/Password:

Date/Password:

Date/Password:

Notes:

Website:

Email:

Username:

Date/Password:

Date/Password:

Date/Password:

Notes:

Website:

Email:

Username:

Date/Password:

Date/Password:

Date/Password:

Notes:

Website:

Email:

Username:

Date/Password:

Date/Password:

Date/Password:

Notes:

Website:

Email:

Username:

Date/Password:

Date/Password:

Date/Password:

Notes:

Website:

Email:

Username:

Date/Password:

Date/Password:

Date/Password:

Notes:

Website:

Email:

Username:

Date/Password:

Date/Password:

Date/Password:

Notes:

P

Website:

Email:

Username:

Date/Password:

Date/Password:

Date/Password:

Notes:

Website:

Email:

Username:

Date/Password:

Date/Password:

Date/Password:

Notes:

Website:

Email:

Username:

Date/Password:

Date/Password:

Date/Password:

Notes:

P

Website:

Email:

Username:

Date/Password:

Date/Password:

Date/Password:

Notes:

Website:

Email:

Username:

Date/Password:

Date/Password:

Date/Password:

Notes:

Website:

Email:

Username:

Date/Password:

Date/Password:

Date/Password:

Notes:

Website:

Email:

Username:

Date/Password:

Date/Password:

Date/Password:

Notes:

Website:

Email:

Username:

Date/Password:

Date/Password:

Date/Password:

Notes:

Website:

Email:

Username:

Date/Password:

Date/Password:

Date/Password:

Notes:

Q

Website:

Email:

Username:

Date/Password:

Date/Password:

Date/Password:

Notes:

Website:

Email:

Username:

Date/Password:

Date/Password:

Date/Password:

Notes:

Website:

Email:

Username:

Date/Password:

Date/Password:

Date/Password:

Notes:

Website:

Email:

Username:

Date/Password:

Date/Password:

Date/Password:

Notes:

Website: _______________________________

Email: _______________________________

Username: _______________________________

Date/Password: _______________________________

Date/Password: _______________________________

Date/Password: _______________________________

Notes: _______________________________

____

Website: _______________________________

Email: _______________________________

Username: _______________________________

Date/Password: _______________________________

Date/Password: _______________________________

Date/Password: _______________________________

Notes: _______________________________

____

Q

Website: _______________________________

Email: _______________________________

Username: _______________________________

Date/Password: _______________________________

Date/Password: _______________________________

Date/Password: _______________________________

Notes: _______________________________

____

R

Website:

Email:

Username:

Date/Password:

Date/Password:

Date/Password:

Notes:

Website:

Email:

Username:

Date/Password:

Date/Password:

Date/Password:

Notes:

Website:

Email:

Username:

Date/Password:

Date/Password:

Date/Password:

Notes:

Website: _______________________

Email: _______________________

Username: _______________________

Date/Password: _______________________

Date/Password: _______________________

Date/Password: _______________________

Notes: _______________________

____

Website: _______________________

Email: _______________________

Username: _______________________

Date/Password: _______________________

Date/Password: _______________________

Date/Password: _______________________

Notes: _______________________

____

Website: _______________________

Email: _______________________

Username: _______________________

Date/Password: _______________________

Date/Password: _______________________

Date/Password: _______________________

Notes: _______________________

____

R

Website: _______________________________

Email: _______________________________

Username: _______________________________

Date/Password: _______________________________

Date/Password: _______________________________

Date/Password: _______________________________

Notes: _______________________________

____

Website: _______________________________

Email: _______________________________

Username: _______________________________

Date/Password: _______________________________

Date/Password: _______________________________

Date/Password: _______________________________

Notes: _______________________________

____

Website: _______________________________

Email: _______________________________

Username: _______________________________

Date/Password: _______________________________

Date/Password: _______________________________

Date/Password: _______________________________

Notes: _______________________________

____

Website:

Email:

Username:

Date/Password:

Date/Password:

Date/Password:

Notes:

Website:

Email:

Username:

Date/Password:

Date/Password:

Date/Password:

Notes:

Website:

Email:

Username:

Date/Password:

Date/Password:

Date/Password:

Notes:

R

Website:

Email:

Username:

Date/Password:

Date/Password:

Date/Password:

Notes:

Website:

Email:

Username:

Date/Password:

Date/Password:

Date/Password:

Notes:

S

Website:

Email:

Username:

Date/Password:

Date/Password:

Date/Password:

Notes:

Website:

Email:

Username:

Date/Password:

Date/Password:

Date/Password:

Notes:

Website:

Email:

Username:

Date/Password:

Date/Password:

Date/Password:

Notes:

Website:

Email:

Username:

Date/Password:

Date/Password:

Date/Password:

Notes:

Website:

Email:

Username:

Date/Password:

Date/Password:

Date/Password:

Notes:

Website:

Email:

Username:

Date/Password:

Date/Password:

Date/Password:

Notes:

S

Website:

Email:

Username:

Date/Password:

Date/Password:

Date/Password:

Notes:

Website:

Email:

Username:

Date/Password:

Date/Password:

Date/Password:

Notes:

Website:

Email:

Username:

Date/Password:

Date/Password:

Date/Password:

Notes:

Website:

Email:

Username:

Date/Password:

Date/Password:

Date/Password:

Notes:

Website:_______________________________________

Email:____

Username:______________________________________

Date/Password:_________________________________

Date/Password:_________________________________

Date/Password:_________________________________

Notes:____

____

Website:_______________________________________

Email:____

Username:______________________________________

Date/Password:_________________________________

Date/Password:_________________________________

Date/Password:_________________________________

Notes:____

____

Website:_______________________________________

Email:____

Username:______________________________________

Date/Password:_________________________________

Date/Password:_________________________________

Date/Password:_________________________________

Notes:____

____

Website:

Email:

Username:

Date/Password:

Date/Password:

Date/Password:

Notes:

Website:

Email:

Username:

Date/Password:

Date/Password:

Date/Password:

Notes:

Website:

Email:

Username:

Date/Password:

Date/Password:

Date/Password:

Notes:

Website: _______________________

Email: _______________________

Username: _______________________

Date/Password: _______________________

Date/Password: _______________________

Date/Password: _______________________

Notes: _______________________

____

Website: _______________________

Email: _______________________

Username: _______________________

Date/Password: _______________________

Date/Password: _______________________

Date/Password: _______________________

Notes: _______________________

____

Website: _______________________

Email: _______________________

Username: _______________________

Date/Password: _______________________

Date/Password: _______________________

Date/Password: _______________________

Notes: _______________________

____

Website:

Email:

Username:

Date/Password:

Date/Password:

Date/Password:

Notes:

Website:

Email:

Username:

Date/Password:

Date/Password:

Date/Password:

Notes:

Website:

Email:

Username:

Date/Password:

Date/Password:

Date/Password:

Notes:

Website: ______________________________________

Email: ______________________________________

Username: ______________________________________

Date/Password: ______________________________________

Date/Password: ______________________________________

Date/Password: ______________________________________

Notes: ______________________________________

____

Website: ______________________________________

Email: ______________________________________

Username: ______________________________________

Date/Password: ______________________________________

Date/Password: ______________________________________

Date/Password: ______________________________________

Notes: ______________________________________

____

Website: ______________________________________

Email: ______________________________________

Username: ______________________________________

Date/Password: ______________________________________

Date/Password: ______________________________________

Date/Password: ______________________________________

Notes: ______________________________________

____

Website:

Email:

Username:

Date/Password:

Date/Password:

Date/Password:

Notes:

Website:

Email:

Username:

Date/Password:

Date/Password:

Date/Password:

Notes:

Website:

Email:

Username:

Date/Password:

Date/Password:

Date/Password:

Notes:

U

Website:

Email:

Username:

Date/Password:

Date/Password:

Date/Password:

Notes:

Website:

Email:

Username:

Date/Password:

Date/Password:

Date/Password:

Notes:

Website:

Email:

Username:

Date/Password:

Date/Password:

Date/Password:

Notes:

Website: ___________________________

Email: ___________________________

Username: ___________________________

Date/Password: ___________________________

Date/Password: ___________________________

Date/Password: ___________________________

Notes: ___________________________

____

Website: ___________________________

Email: ___________________________

Username: ___________________________

Date/Password: ___________________________

Date/Password: ___________________________

Date/Password: ___________________________

Notes: ___________________________

____

Website: ___________________________

Email: ___________________________

Username: ___________________________

Date/Password: ___________________________

Date/Password: ___________________________

Date/Password: ___________________________

Notes: ___________________________

____

Website:

Email:

Username:

Date/Password:

Date/Password:

Date/Password:

Notes:

Website:

Email:

Username:

Date/Password:

Date/Password:

Date/Password:

Notes:

Website:

Email:

Username:

Date/Password:

Date/Password:

Date/Password:

Notes:

Website:

Email:

Username:

Date/Password:

Date/Password:

Date/Password:

Notes:

Website:

Email:

Username:

Date/Password:

Date/Password:

Date/Password:

Notes:

Website:

Email:

Username:

Date/Password:

Date/Password:

Date/Password:

Notes:

Website:

Email:

Username:

Date/Password:

Date/Password:

Date/Password:

Notes:

Website:

Email:

Username:

Date/Password:

Date/Password:

Date/Password:

Notes:

Website:

Email:

Username:

Date/Password:

Date/Password:

Date/Password:

Notes:

Website:

Email:

Username:

Date/Password:

Date/Password:

Date/Password:

Notes:

Website:

Email:

Username:

Date/Password:

Date/Password:

Date/Password:

Notes:

Website:

Email:

Username:

Date/Password:

Date/Password:

Date/Password:

Notes:

V

Website:

Email:

Username:

Date/Password:

Date/Password:

Date/Password:

Notes:

Website:

Email:

Username:

Date/Password:

Date/Password:

Date/Password:

Notes:

Website:

Email:

Username:

Date/Password:

Date/Password:

Date/Password:

Notes:

Website:

Email:

Username:

Date/Password:

Date/Password:

Date/Password:

Notes:

Website:

Email:

Username:

Date/Password:

Date/Password:

Date/Password:

Notes:

Website:

Email:

Username:

Date/Password:

Date/Password:

Date/Password:

Notes:

Website:

Email:

Username:

Date/Password:

Date/Password:

Date/Password:

Notes:

Website:

Email:

Username:

Date/Password:

Date/Password:

Date/Password:

Notes:

Website:

Email:

Username:

Date/Password:

Date/Password:

Date/Password:

Notes:

Website:

Email:

Username:

Date/Password:

Date/Password:

Date/Password:

Notes:

Website:

Email:

Username:

Date/Password:

Date/Password:

Date/Password:

Notes:

Website:

Email:

Username:

Date/Password:

Date/Password:

Date/Password:

Notes:

Website:

Email:

Username:

Date/Password:

Date/Password:

Date/Password:

Notes:

Website:

Email:

Username:

Date/Password:

Date/Password:

Date/Password:

Notes:

Website:

Email:

Username:

Date/Password:

Date/Password:

Date/Password:

Notes:

Website: _______________________________

Email: _______________________________

Username: _______________________________

Date/Password: _______________________________

Date/Password: _______________________________

Date/Password: _______________________________

Notes: _______________________________

____

Website: _______________________________

Email: _______________________________

Username: _______________________________

Date/Password: _______________________________

Date/Password: _______________________________

Date/Password: _______________________________

Notes: _______________________________

____

Website: _______________________________

Email: _______________________________

Username: _______________________________

Date/Password: _______________________________

Date/Password: _______________________________

Date/Password: _______________________________

Notes: _______________________________

____

Website:

Email:

Username:

Date/Password:

Date/Password:

Date/Password:

Notes:

Website:

Email:

Username:

Date/Password:

Date/Password:

Date/Password:

Notes:

Website:

Email:

Username:

Date/Password:

Date/Password:

Date/Password:

Notes:

Website:

Email:

Username:

Date/Password:

Date/Password:

Date/Password:

Notes:

Website:

Email:

Username:

Date/Password:

Date/Password:

Date/Password:

Notes:

Website:

Email:

Username:

Date/Password:

Date/Password:

Date/Password:

Notes:

X

Website:

Email:

Username:

Date/Password:

Date/Password:

Date/Password:

Notes:

Website:

Email:

Username:

Date/Password:

Date/Password:

Date/Password:

Notes:

Website:

Email:

Username:

Date/Password:

Date/Password:

Date/Password:

Notes:

Website:____________________________

Email:______________________________

Username:___________________________

Date/Password:______________________

Date/Password:______________________

Date/Password:______________________

Notes:______________________________

____

Website:____________________________

Email:______________________________

Username:___________________________

Date/Password:______________________

Date/Password:______________________

Date/Password:______________________

Notes:______________________________

____

Website:____________________________

Email:______________________________

Username:___________________________

Date/Password:______________________

Date/Password:______________________

Date/Password:______________________

Notes:______________________________

____

Website: _______________________
Email: _______________________
Username: _______________________
Date/Password: _______________________
Date/Password: _______________________
Date/Password: _______________________
Notes: _______________________
____

Website: _______________________
Email: _______________________
Username: _______________________
Date/Password: _______________________
Date/Password: _______________________
Date/Password: _______________________
Notes: _______________________
____

Website: _______________________
Email: _______________________
Username: _______________________
Date/Password: _______________________
Date/Password: _______________________
Date/Password: _______________________
Notes: _______________________
____

Website: ____

Email: ____

Username: ____

Date/Password: ____

Date/Password: ____

Date/Password: ____

Notes: ____

____

Website: ____

Email: ____

Username: ____

Date/Password: ____

Date/Password: ____

Date/Password: ____

Notes: ____

____

Website: ____

Email: ____

Username: ____

Date/Password: ____

Date/Password: ____

Date/Password: ____

Notes: ____

____

Y

A B C D E F G H I J K L M N O P Q R S T U V W X Y **Z**

Website:

Email:

Username:

Date/Password:

Date/Password:

Date/Password:

Notes:

Website:

Email:

Username:

Date/Password:

Date/Password:

Date/Password:

Notes:

Website:

Email:

Username:

Date/Password:

Date/Password:

Date/Password:

Notes:

Website: ____

Email: ____

Username: ____

Date/Password: ____

Date/Password: ____

Date/Password: ____

Notes: ____

____

Website: ____

Email: ____

Username: ____

Date/Password: ____

Date/Password: ____

Date/Password: ____

Notes: ____

____

Website: ____

Email: ____

Username: ____

Date/Password: ____

Date/Password: ____

Date/Password: ____

Notes: ____

____

Website:
Email:
Username:
Date/Password:
Date/Password:
Date/Password:
Notes:

Website:
Email:
Username:
Date/Password:
Date/Password:
Date/Password:
Notes:

Website:
Email:
Username:
Date/Password:
Date/Password:
Date/Password:
Notes:

Website:

Email:

Username:

Date/Password:

Date/Password:

Date/Password:

Notes:

Website:

Email:

Username:

Date/Password:

Date/Password:

Date/Password:

Notes:

Website:

Email:

Username:

Date/Password:

Date/Password:

Date/Password:

Notes:

NOTES

NOTES

Made in the USA
Monee, IL
07 July 2026

56551518R00066